shaping the flame

foreword

The arts no longer communicate through symbols, metaphysics, or through the world of the divine imagination. We are in the grips of a disease which has its origins in a defection of the mind which can only be cured by a change of mind, a looking God-wards, and a remaking of ourselves. The fact that *'shaping the flame'* exists at all in this secularist, materialist junkyard is indeed remarkable.

If our civilisation is not going to sink, like the Titanic, we are empowered to reinstate the sacred not only into our art, but also into every aspect of our lives. This would indeed be a Beatitude, a move towards a divine art, where one could say with Dante *"All my thoughts speak of love"*, divine love which is the source of all harmony and infinitude.

It is toward this 'harmony' that *'shaping the flame'* points in all its plenitude.

John Tavener

Composer

Dedicated to the Special Child in all of us. Revealing a veiled path,
flowers amidst thorns, a flame that kindles warmth,
a bird's wing that embraces the heart,
a handful of creativity, footsteps in the spiralling stars of eternity.

MV

Summer Light Wool Weaving

St John's

Space

Architecture

Basket-making Spring

Autumn

Pottery Carnival

Harvest

Animal Kingdom Drama

the Inner Metal
Earth Care Path Passion
the Week
Candlemas Individual Social Forming
Art
Corpus Easter
Seeds Christi Michaelmas

Epiphany Baking
the Land Wood

Holy Nights *Community-building* Therapies
Whitsun Clay
Music Herbs
Dance Stone
Christmas Healing
Eurythmy All Saints
Ascension and All Souls
Painting

Kingdoms Coloured Glass
of Life
Martinmas
Advent
Winter
Candle-making

Lighting the Flame

Every journey has a beginning, but not necessarily an end.

This is the beginning of the journey that is *shaping the flame* but it does not conclude with the final page of this book. It is a journey of life and creativity - an artistic journey through the seasons and festivals of the year with the people who live in Camphill communities in all parts of the world. The journey will continue with them, and you, into the future after this book is closed. So let us now set out at the beginning, in Arlesheim, Switzerland, just before Christmas, 1927.

It is the first Sunday of Advent, and Karl König, a young Viennese doctor, is invited to a celebration at the Sonnenhof - the 'House of the Sun' - a home for children with special needs. He is the guest of Ita Wegman, a doctor whose life is inspired by the Austrian philosopher, Rudolf Steiner.

They enter a room lit only by a single large candle, perched on a small hillock of logs, moss, ivy and crystals, at the centre of a large spiral of moss that has been laid out on the floor with great care. This is an Advent Garden and, as Dr König's eyes accustom to the candle-light, he makes out, nestling in the soft moss at the entrance to the spiral, an array of shiny red apples, each holding an unlit candle backed by a fresh sprig of fir.

To an accompaniment of gentle carols and the ethereal strains of lyres, each of the children present, in turn, picks up an apple and makes his or her way to the middle of the spiral. Here, they light their candle from the central flame. Turning, they retrace their steps, faces illuminated by the light they hold, to place the burning candle at a point of their own choosing. Slowly, as one child after another completes the journey, the spiral brightens, glowing with ever increasing light.

Some children participate unaided, while others need help and guidance on the long path to the centre and back again. Each journey is unique, a metaphor for creation, birth, the passage through life. The room is imbued with reverence and wonder, a mood to kindle awe and compassion, and such, indeed, is the effect on Karl König.

Through the following twelve years the flame lit that day grows ever brighter. War has engulfed Europe, and Dr. König is first homeless, then a refugee, and eventually settles in Scotland. He places his candle in the spiral of life on a small estate near Aberdeen, called Camphill, and there an original form of community-living takes root. Over time, the social ideas grow, and more communities are formed in which volunteer co-workers, and children, young people and adults with special needs, live together in an atmosphere where the dignity of every human being is upheld and can thrive.

At the heart of each community are the celebration of the Christian Festivals, care for the earth, care for each other and respect for the spirit in each one where education, arts, crafts and therapies can develop and grow. This vision, and its manifestation in the many Camphill communities formed around the world, is the inspiration for the poetic and visual imagery presented in *shaping the flame*.

This is an extraordinary story told in an unusual way. Many pages shine out colourfully. Others are quieter. Some, perhaps, are a little obscure.

Dip in. Reflect on what you find. Muse over it.

There are reminders of childhood, and times when life and art become entwined - of uplifting moments and turning to new thoughts and deeds. If it manages to refresh and nourish in some deeper way, its purpose is fulfilled.

There are windows on to a world of imagination, with subjects and themes linked in unconventional ways. Be guided on this journey of discovery by the *Dove*, the *Flame*, the *Stars* and other key images which are introduced in the pages which follow.

The Dove and the Flame

The *Dove* is an image of the pure eternal spirit within every person, and of beauty and innocence, ready to descend into our pressured world with a promise to us all - like the picture of the dove returning to Noah with the olive branch in its beak.

The *Flame* represents the powers of life, enthusiasm and love at the heart of each of us, vulnerable, yet yearning to reach ever upwards.

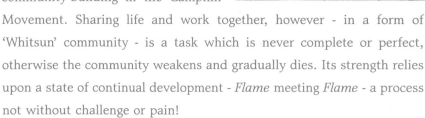

The *realities* behind the *Dove* and the *Flame* entwine, working together to find mutual expression and enhancement and to face fundamental questions of meaning and morality.

Our artistic, creative impulse is born of this synthesis.

The image of the *Dove*, descending, and the active, striving *Flame* of the individual has inspired co-workers to dedicate themselves to community-building in the Camphill

Movement. Sharing life and work together, however - in a form of 'Whitsun' community - is a task which is never complete or perfect, otherwise the community weakens and gradually dies. Its strength relies upon a state of continual development - *Flame* meeting *Flame* - a process not without challenge or pain!

This is the core of life in Camphill: the 'social art', building community through the creative interaction of *Dove* and *Flame*.

But how do we connect to the eternal in the other?

In the image of the *Stars*, we reach out with our aspirations, our hopes and dreams, even our restless determination, to discover ourselves and be true to our worth and potential.

The expression of the struggles and joys that we experience, as we search for an answer, is the universal 'language' found in the arts and the crafts, and in the celebration of the festivals. The artistic can help us to deeper appreciation and understanding. We keep our *Flame* active through art and social interaction.

This artistic language allows us to begin, no matter how clumsily, to "...*speak to the stars*..." and so to recognise the aspirations, hopes and dreams of others.

These two verses capture the essence of this quest:

> *The stars spake once to Man.*
> *It is World-destiny*
> *That they are silent now.*
> *To be aware of the silence*
> *Can become pain for earthly Man.*
>
> *But in the deepening silence*
> *There grows and ripens*
> *What Man speaks to the Stars.*
> *To be aware of the speaking*
> *Can become strength for Spirit-Man.*
>
> RS

> *Could I but kindle everyman*
> *With the spirit of the cosmos*
> *That he might be a flame*
> *And unfold his being's essence as a flame*
> *Others would take water from the cosmos*
> *To quench the flame*
> *And make all being*
> *Watery dull within.*
> *Oh joy, to see the human flame*
> *Burning brightly, even when at rest!*
> *Oh bitterness, to see Man like a thing*
> *Bound where he would be free.*
>
> RS

Themes on the Journey of 'shaping the flame'

Other images join the *Dove*, *Flame* and *Stars* to act as companions and signs on the journey.

The *Spiral* indicates flow and movement: the changing path of the sun, the flow of the seasons, the movement between birth, death, and renewal. It also portrays the cycle of the Christian festivals, which we instinctively link to the rhythms of nature, as they are created anew each time they are celebrated. Throughout the journey, the festivals and seasons are portrayed mainly from a northern viewpoint. The relationships are quite different in the southern hemisphere.

The Breathing Earth is a picture we carry within us like a seed of hope, a memory of Eden. Bursting forth during summer and resting during winter, in a form of 'cosmic breathing', the earth is a living entity whose harmonious vitality sustains our human existence at every level - not just the physical. We sense the breathing earth when we work in the gardens and on the land. In this picture, the elements of warmth, light, water and soil can once again become pure and untarnished, nurturing forces of wonder, beauty and compassion.

The *Portraits* of people living in Camphill centres, mainly in the British Isles, sometimes further afield, represent the boundless and unique potential of each individual - the essence of humanity.

The *Path* of destiny that each of us must walk is our own, with ups and downs, searches and struggles, and there are *Thresholds* - bridges to cross, doorways, gates - especially other people!

A *Sense of Place* positions us on this Earth and allows our lives to take shape. Our *Hands* grasp the substance of life and are used in our endeavours, working in the home and on the land, engaging in the arts and crafts. We act on the world and the world acts on us - forming, blessing, receiving.

These images and themes, plus brief explanations on the way, are pointers on our journey, and with them in our minds, we are ready to set out.

Heights of Summer
Descending to Hearth and Home

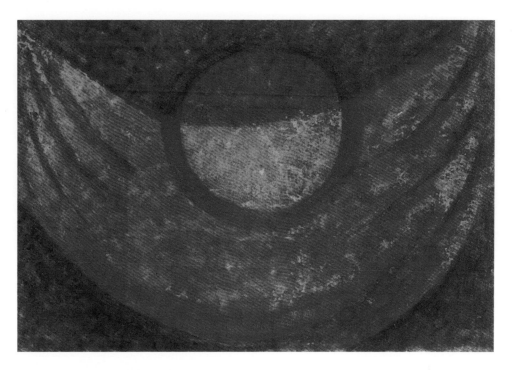

We join the spiral of the year when the sun in the north is at its zenith, the days at their longest, the world full of warmth and light, the exhilaration of growth sweeping us along on a tide of beauty, the first fruits ripening.

Just past mid-summer, on the twenty-fourth of June, we celebrate the festival of St John the Baptist - the selfless witness to the coming of Christ - with the image of the transforming fire, confronting us with questions of how true we are to our inner power of conscience. Will we respond to the challenge - as the sun, at its solstice, stands guard, showing the way to the inner sun of consciousness?

It is a time of year when we can feel opened up, even exposed. On our journey, we encounter the crafts of wool and weaving cloth, the activities of building and home-making, and places which give covering and protection in preparation for the coming Autumn and Michaelmas.

Summer Warmth

Tall brick wall,
  course on course
laid patiently,
and on it the shadow
of a poplar flickers,
  dark flame
    rippling
      over the bricks,
        waiting to be
          beautiful.

Slowly the grape grows sweet, and wheat
will swell with sun and rain to keep
my body strong, my soul alive,
oh, give thanks my soul alive.

the earth breathes

Summer in the city,

    sharp shadows on smart squares

       and dreams on dusty wasteland.

        Lovers touch on street corners

        and old men tend geraniums,

        warmth making them one with the world.

        Sun, loving, making us bubble

        and the first cherries drip crimson.

        But under concrete, under slabs,

        remember the parched earth, speechless,

        how it must heave and ache

        to be free to reach the sky.

        And in city hearts, made dry by life,

        a dead shell cracks open in the heat.

The Light of Summer

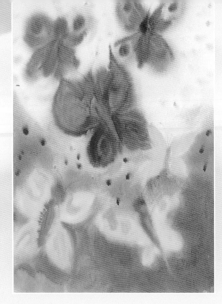

light condensing to a bundle of wool

We have travelled far

since the only light

was the one midnight candle.

Glimpses of paradise

by Christmas fires

stirred us into journey

as pilgrims to the starry fields,

rising as the sun grew stronger,

earth's breath lifting us

here to the father's home,

this pool which swallows flame

and shadow,

turns water into light;

this singing sea which takes us out of time

and shows us to eternity.

through finger and thumb runs the twisted thread,

The shearer must be a man of muscle but let him be a quiet one too,
so the ewe will sit easy, lean against him and let the wool come soft as butter from the pat.
For if he's tight, or hasty, then she's a struggle and it's nothing but blood and tears.
Shearing's hard toil, the hardest, it would make Saint Peter sweat, but in the right hands it's peaceful work,
letting the ewe spring away, naked and skinny, while you tuck up the fleece
and toss it towards winter.

gossamer filaments spun silky thin, gently stretched, teased and turned to endless yarn

Patterns weaving dreams

Songs of daily want

Wheel of Fortune   Honeysuckle

Cloth for the newborn

to hold her tight

in this wide world

Rosepath   Sunrise

Shawl for the bride

that her beauty

shall be covered

Pine Bloom   Butternut

Warmth for the mother

to cover thin shoulders

when the wind bites

Snail's Trail   Bowknot

Cover for the body

over which we watch

while life is leaving

Chariot Wheel   Monk's Belt

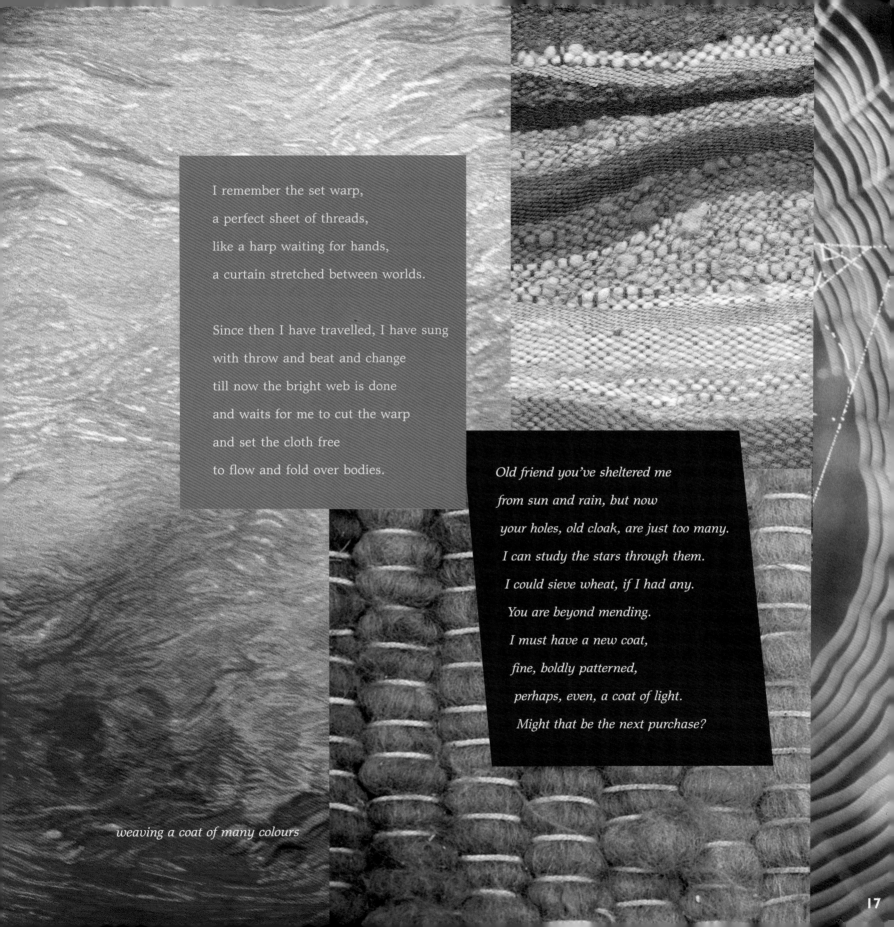

I remember the set warp,

a perfect sheet of threads,

like a harp waiting for hands,

a curtain stretched between worlds.

Since then I have travelled, I have sung

with throw and beat and change

till now the bright web is done

and waits for me to cut the warp

and set the cloth free

to flow and fold over bodies.

Old friend you've sheltered me

from sun and rain, but now

your holes, old cloak, are just too many.

I can study the stars through them.

I could sieve wheat, if I had any.

You are beyond mending.

I must have a new coat,

fine, boldly patterned,

perhaps, even, a coat of light.

Might that be the next purchase?

weaving a coat of many colours

17

Sin.

We shy away from such a little word.

Call it a mistake, a debt,

Something which I saw too late,

For which .... apologies.

Then John's eyes burn into us,

Showing us how we send pain

Hunting for a place to catch and grow,

Begging us to change, to rise to life.

Mother, I do not know

if I tremble, or does

the earth still shake

as it did by the river.

We went to see John,

to see the flames that

come from his mouth,

the lion at his feet asleep.

Then a man came

and all went quiet.

John led him down into the water

and then he let God

loose among us

and the world was

shadowed in glory

and I was shaking, Mother,

shaking.

Our cruel deeds

Left to fester

Would choke the world,

Leave it wrecked, dark.

O flame, o faithful flame,

Free all that shut hurt.

Fire of truth,

Fire of love,

take pains and

make good

change your thinking...
...urges the inner voice of conscience

In the head the power of faith,

In the heart the might of love,

In the full human being all-sustaining hope.

RS

Living Spaces

drawing a line

To
begin the web the spider
floats a thread and lets it fall,
following to secure it. Then she completes a
triangle of threads, returning via another point to
the place when she began. Then, in careful order,
crossing the growing circle to and fro, she spins the
spokes of what becomes a wheel within a triangle.
Then from its centre she spins a spiral outward
round the spokes. This spiral is a scaffold. It will
go when the fine sticky beaded threads
between the spokes have been
completed. Now she must sit
and wait.

capturing space

*From Java to Greenland
men sit by fires, talking of rain,
hoping for good luck.*

*The Inuit makes a circle,
cuts big wedges of snow
to build an igloo,
spiralling dome,
the cracks between the blocks
glowing in the night.*

*The Bedouin, far from water,
must welcome his enemy
to share his camp.
Before prayers
they wash their hands
with clean, dry sand.*

*The Masai settle
with the rains,
a season for song
and ceremony.
The women build a hut
for blessing of the elders.*

Places for Working and Learning

Each day we must build this room anew, give it windows as before, but today let them open with a different slant reaching further into the world or allowing the eye to be rested by green trees or water flowing. From this spot we can see stars or walk with Pharaohs or sail oceans with spices from the East. Here we work, here

we learn, here we see, here we listen to the world. We return each day to the same place, we do not begin from scratch. This is where we know we must meet, must embark again. The windows must be set straight, the light let in, and our song be ready to fly beyond the walls, through these windows we have opened wide.

The day begins with the key turning the lock,
still stiff from night's inactivity.
The workers take up tools once again,
approach each other
with careful jokes.

At the end, the slow persistent broom
sweeps up the fragments of the day,
clay or cloth or sawdust.
For this is a shop, a workshop,
which takes what has been dug, cut, spun,
all that is raw,
and handles it to man's desire.

Here people rub shoulders,
hands move in noise and silence,
the sawdust dances,
the needle snakes,
the clay curves
to give us stool and cup and coat,
or a doll with just a hint of a face
ready to be made whole by love.

From here men and women
go home satisfied,
peaceful from the love
that is as solid
as the dust dancing in the air.

I was glad of the walk from the station,

up the long hill out of town,

and then down into the valley where the house stood surrounded by trees.

An impression of white among dark.   A stranger would not know it was there.

This was me coming home.

As I got nearer it all seemed so

impossibly tangible, each tree

awake, each shadow known; this

place of nurture remembering me.

I stood at a distance and looked

at the house. It held my life.

I thought of the long path

that had led me back to

its mystery,

its bright face.

a place to be

safe and warm

The child traces raindrops

down the window pane,

thinking of nothing

She leans on the table

her womb so full and heavy,

wondering when

She stirs the sauce,

talking gently to her friend

while thick bubbles rise and burst

A tangled mass of kittens,

asleep and feeding,

the mother cat inert, purring

She strokes the book

before she opens it,

feeling voices waiting

The cake sits cooling

and makes the whole house

cake-shaped

The harvest has come, the days shorten, and the dying-away that marks autumn - with its flaming colours and meteor showers - begins to give us fresh stimulation. The traveller has returned, heart still filled with summer's warmth, ready to settle down and work.

At the equinox there is a moment of equilibrium as daytime matches night - a threshold. Then the north grows darker as the south begins an upsurge of growth, life and hope. The sun can still be warm, but there is chill in the morning air. We are aware of the stars in the night sky again after the long days of summer.

The twenty-ninth of September is the festival of Michaelmas, celebrating the mighty angelic being from a world beyond our normal consciousness. St Michael can give us courage to face the coming cold and darkness, the challenges that befall us. Many artists have depicted St Michael sitting upon a white steed, clad with a red mantle, with sword or spear holding the 'dragon' at bay - an image that can restore harmony, if we so wish, whenever we experience fear or chaos.

It is the moment to reflect on how our inner thoughts compare with our active participation in life, perhaps to discover new insights or directions. This is a subtle process which belongs to autumn and to those crafts in which we shape, mould and carve the materials of the earth - the modelling of clay, the chiselling of stone, the sanding of wood, the hammering of hot metal.

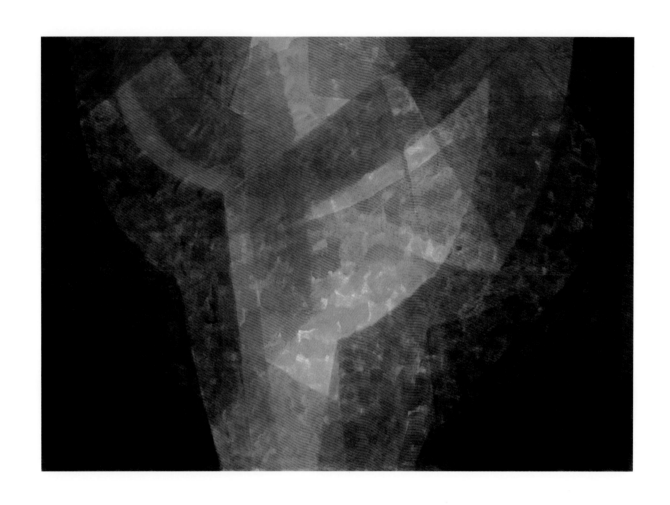

light and dark

Colours Turning

Walking in the Autumn dawn

over the first earth turned

brown and gleaming by the plough,

I hear the stags challenging,

the red stags rutting in the scrub.

Bracken is turning to umber

and dock heads are dark as blood clots.

The stags bellow

a time for reformation,

for the wind to come and strip the trees

and make us all stand naked creatures

under the buzzard's circling eye.

The old moon is setting;

the Earth is older and needs

more than moon sleep of silver dreams

in order to be made anew.

There is a clash and clatter

as the dawn turns a golden rose.

Above the free flowing stream

bright leaves hang,

a moment from falling,

to float,

drift,

sink,

lodge,

crumble to detritus,

a feast of waste,

the source of life unseen.

Now they just hang, in Autumn,

crisp and fierce against the blue,

possessing my eyes,

vivid as flames.

Take the narrow path
across slow waves of wheat,
rusty ripe and glittering
with dew as day rises.
I brush the heavy heads
and scatter drops of water
on the early air.
All creation caught
in the gleam of grain
ready for the blade.

Glowing Metals

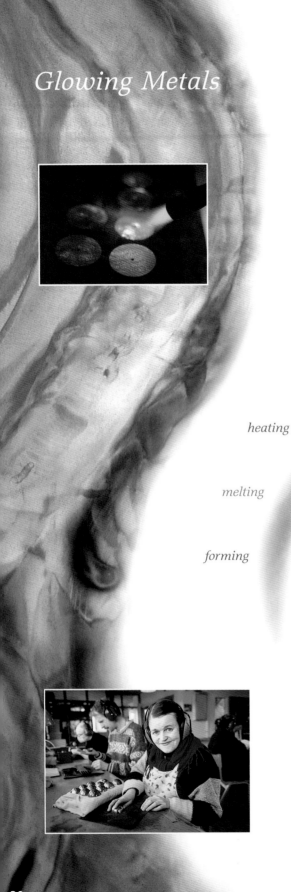

Let me explain. You see, I work in a workshop that
makes Christmas Tree signs, in copper. Not many
people know about Christmas Tree signs. It's hard to
explain. Some people want a pretty tree and some want
a beautiful tree: a tree that's alive, a tree with
meaning. The tree with tinsel and coloured balls is
lovely, but it's only pretty. The tree with signs is
precious. There are signs for sun and moon, and the
planets, and for the coming down to earth from
heaven. On top there's a delicate five-pointed star.
That's a hard one to cut, and file and beat and polish.
There's one, for our human nature, that's
a square connected to a triangle
above. It took me a long time to like

heating

glowing
that one: but now I think of all the
square things that we use, but we love to look

melting
up to the mountains. When they are on the tree it is like the

flowing
universe and the signs are floating light - but hard.

forming
Once at Christmas I was somewhere where they had no signs.
I told them about the signs and the people made some.
Out of dough. Out of bread. We had no copper.
They were all right. A golden colour, fresh and alive.
But so are the copper ones; they're alive too in a waiting sort
of way. When we're sick of cutting and being neat, and tired
of the noise and the polishing, then we make enamel;
ground rock crystal and metals melted. We make angels
and you see how the metals melt and glow and flow.
Jewels. It looks like creation - and so does the tree,
with our signs of life shining in the green.

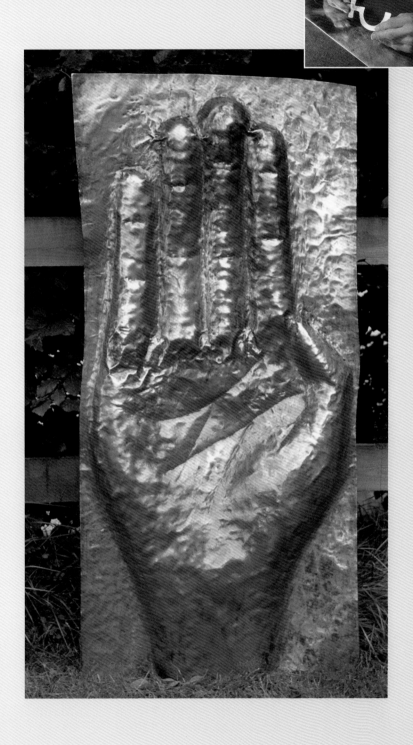

Iron - fire freed you from broken stone to give us steam and steel. Iron - made in stars from the first fire waiting to be moulded, flowing in our blood, iron wherever there must be give and take of life's energy, fetching and carrying, there you are, magnanimous, ready to be used for good or ill, obedient iron.

In the Hebrides at Michaelmas people would play games of stealing horses, leaving only the old nag if they could. The demand of Michael was to fly free, to circle the world, to rise above nature. No matter who owns her, each man or woman had need of the boldest steed.

Michaelmas

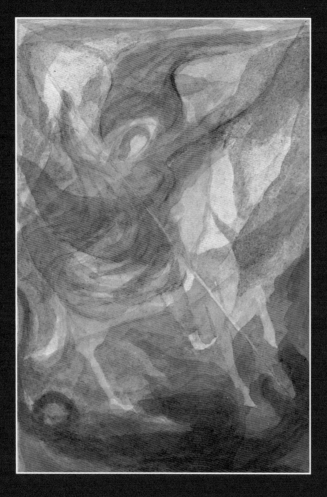

First the pink unbroken bud

becomes an open bloom

and then the petals fall.

O crimson rose

now among the stars,

your colour in my blood,

I will go out to find you.

Sometimes I have dragon's eyes,

  cold and knowing,

    face pressed close to the dust,

    seeing just surfaces.

      O let me have dove's eyes,

        the diving dove who sees the sky,

        the clear waters below,

          whose flame is inside, singular,

          not burning as the dragon's deadly breath.

          Whose face will lead my eyes

            to find the purer earth? The angel Michael.

          If I can meet his clear gaze

          then I will light upon

          my Christ road,

          my needle's eye.

facing challenges

In the free being of Man

The Universe is gathered up.

Then in the free resolve of your heart

Take your own life in hand,

And you will find the World.

The Spirit of the World will find itself in you.

RS

33

ART
STUDIO

Qualities of Wood

Those planks of ash are from the tree that
stood by the bee hives. Think back.
Once this would have made a plough,
a heavy plough, shaped, resilient, the team
of oxen hauling it, labouring through the
stones, the bitter clay. Back-breaking work.
Or a spear, ash has made spears right back
to Homer and beyond, flexible, quivering
through the air like a shaft of sunlight.
No such simple slaughter any more.
Or it could become an oar for slave or
freeman, Viking raider or a gentleman on
the Thames, taking the strain of wave or
current. But I will make a ladder with this
wood, for picking apples and clearing
gutters or rescuing a cat, or just to climb
to look out over the world, the world we
have been given, the world we have made.
I will make a ladder of the fallen ash.

You make tables don't you? ... We need a table, or two tables, or three, we're not sure! ... Dining tables, but we want to do other things on them, too ... oh, you know, games and making things and thinking. ... Yes, a table helps with thinking. I like that lovely white wood there ... it's holly? ... that's funny, holly's so green and red isn't it? ... and on the inside it's so white. You'd never know. We couldn't have our tables made of ... no, I see, it's rare, good for bowls. ... That is a lovely colour, that piece, all rippling ... it's walnut? That's very posh, isn't it? ... we couldn't have ... no, thousands, you say, from the Black Sea. ... We don't want it oblong, too much pass your plates and did you hear me. We're a community, you see, quite a room full, it can get very noisy. ... I like the sound of lime ... that's lime, is it? but ... but it's a leg, a wooden leg ... your grandfather's! No! ... How interesting, a lion. ... We wondered about hexagonal or octagonal. The one with eight sides. Better than a circle ... for passing the ketchup. ... That's beautiful ... elm, you say ... for your grandfather's ... coffin? ... He wants to go out in style. ... What about one of those kits from Denmark? ... you could help us with the instructions. ... I'll see myself out ... oops, sorry ... why, bless me, it's another one ... another wooden leg ... really? amazing! ...

yew   ash   cherry   oak   elm   maple   birch

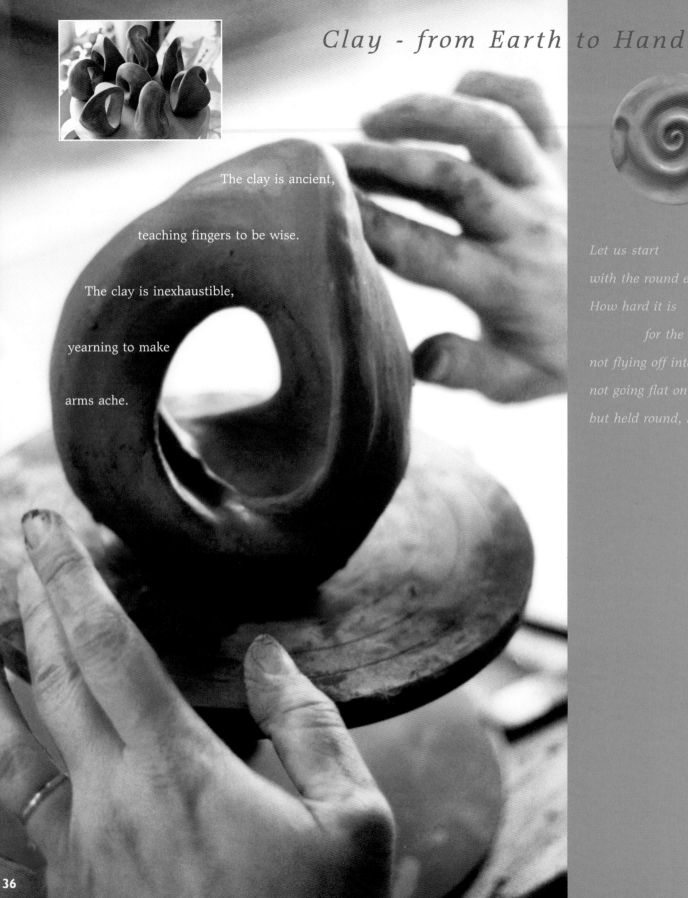

The clay is ancient,

teaching fingers to be wise.

The clay is inexhaustible,

yearning to make

arms ache.

Let us start
with the round earth.
How hard it is
        for the Earth to be round,
not flying off into space,
not going flat on us,
but held round, homely.

digging

kneading

pressing

forming

shaping

modelling

We work the dough,

we press the clay.

Shaping, we think;

moulding, we know.

I will build you a man,

pile mass on mass,

give enough weight

to do justice to his spirit

so that he is well protected,

but fertile, eager to be free,

to be free.

Ancient Stone

We shape, we construct, we learn to handle matter - brittle sandstone, impenetrable granite. We serve it, we work it, perhaps we master it - see that window where the mason has made flames of the tracery - each time I take a chisel I shape my life, my insides. However far I travel with my skill, whatever my privileges, the secret is mine. I know how truly I have struck the stone, how worthy of the trade of making self my life has been.

the bones of the earth

Grip the chisel, angle it,
Strike for chip and spark.
Stone, slowly the
water would
dissolve you,
hard rain
and gentle,
then we could
drink you in,
but I must go
quicker,
while life is
in me,
to find your life,
the body
down inside you, stone.
Carve the element and wrap it
in a skin of cut light.

The marble slab is rubbed smooth
and dappled rose with veins of ancient life.
The mason is measuring letters
for the one who has died - name, dates,
a blessing and a wish.
Now it is an S for which the rule is put by.
The chisel chips tiny fragments
for the serpent letter, following its life
scribed on the surface,
marking the silence of the stone.
A lark rises by him where he works
in the air of day.
She lifts her body into the blue,
singing for the stone,
for the love in the mallet,
for the true naming of man
that will stand in the weather
and will slowly be softened
by moss and the salt sea wind.
Little by little
she lifts
the measure
to heaven.

A Time of Expectancy

November, often a period of gloom and storm. Though southern lands are carpeted in flowers, fallen leaves decay over the earth's surface in the north. Damp and cold creep into our northern lives.

The log-fire burns. A candle is lit. As the light of day decreases, a mood of patient expectation arises, allowing the colours of the soul to be perceived more clearly by our inner eye.

In the lighting of a simple candle we show our wish to recognise and protect something wise and eternal in each of us. Our thoughts are drawn to those who have crossed 'over the threshold'. It is the time of Remembrance, of All Saints and All Souls. While we cultivate this inner quiet we also become more sensitive and responsive to others, as the festival of St Martin expresses.

On the eleventh day of November we celebrate Martinmas. Coloured lanterns, glowing with candlelight, hang among the dying leaves or they are carried in processions, accompanied by songs and pageants. These remind us of the inspiring life of St Martin, the 'soldier turned Bishop'. It is a time for sharing our own 'cloak' of plenty.

Our journey now turns to the arts and crafts where flowing colours speak - glass-staining, candle-making, painting and the world of colours. Each now has a space in which to shine and glow.

Soon, we enter the holy space of Advent. Along its spiralling path we may contemplate the wonders of creation, the gradual incarnation, the mid-winter birth of the Christ Child.

Threshold Crossing

It is autumn in the north,

the days are short,

the months numbered to decline

to dark December.

Feel a second Easter,

underground, below our minds,

teaching us about living with the dead.

All Saints, All Souls,

festivals of resurrection -

when wet and heavy

hang the dying flowers;

but in southern lands

these days break on us

with green as sharp as a healing blade.

The family gathers,

shares cake and wine

with strangers who go by.

They picnic by the grave

though the day is chilly;

a few daisies still to pick

and thread together as a chain

for the youngest grandchild.

Last year he was here,

this year not - grandfather -

but the family makes the circle,

like the stars, the flowers

on the young one's breast.

Around them, sparrows

bicker for the crumbs

and overhead

white doves wheel in the blue.

Sit here in this space,

this place of prayer.

To the west

the round window

of the sun going down

in the sea of the living.

To the east

the thin window

of the dawn

in the garden of hope.

Sit here and be as still

as water where clouds

pass reflected.

Take them in, both,

the tall thin window

and the coloured flower

and marry them,

dazzling lance and evening rose

glowing in the body

of this calm ship of stone

taking us to seas unknown.

Looking Through

from grains to flow

from grit to clear

from formless comes the curve

from mass to thin

from vast to ring

from restless sand comes glass

light

silica

fire

glass

Light must shine on something
or else it is not seen.
All is dark in emptiness.
Be thankful for the stain -
cobalt, manganese, copper, tin -
peculiar strains of earth
giving body to the glass,
giving body to the light,
immaculate light, let it in,
let the light come to the dark house.
Emmanuel!
God with us!
Invisible no more.

a wondrous substance

protective

transparent bridge between one world and another

Martinmas

It is four hundred years since the life of Christ. Vandals surge across the frozen Rhine, the Goths stamp at the gates of Rome. The classical world collapsing into dark ages. It was then that Martin came, the last soldier of Rome, obedient, poor, chaste, packed off to the army by his father angry at the boy's love of religion. By the end of his life you find a thousand men, like sand martins, in caves by the River Loire, living the discipline of Martin. His long life is caught in the deed of sharing, when he met the beggar at the city gate and cut his cloak in two. The bystanders laughed. They did not recognise the stranger Christ. Eight hundred years later another angry father, Pietro Bernadone, in the Piazza del Commune, in Assisi, saw his son, Francis, the poverello, strip off all his clothes. His cloak, the whole of it, he had already given to a poor knight. From Martin we learn sharing, from Francis the unconditional gift. We need to know both, how to give and how to share, for both are healing, both kindle the light which lets us see the meaning in our lives.

sharing a cloak of warmth

I will take my flame

out into the dark and the wind.

It will be safe inside

the bright lantern I have made.

Look out for me

coming through the starry night!

Winter White

from upstream
you might miss it,
the quiet river swells
between thick evergreens
suddenly to plunge

from downstream
the ravine closes in,
the sound grows,
the river bends
and you face the wall of rock,
the waterfall

that's winter,
sometimes flood and force,
sometimes ice and mist;
one day creeping up on us,
numbing,
another, opening us to cold glory

The sheep feast

among the heather,

fresh on the bare hill,

winter's juicy pickings.

I wish there were birches there,

not just the low wiry life,

soft birches, purple and silver,

helping us to be tender,

to remember paradise

when the world is bleak

and winter turns us cruel

wakefulness within the depths

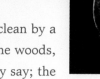

a good year for pine cones. Walking through the old wood a cone drops at my feet, picked clean by a crossbill, each bract bent back and the seeds prised out. What a strange bird, a parrot of the pine woods, with its red feathers, its crossed bill. He tried to pull the nails from the hands of Christ, they say; the effort bent his bill and bloodied his plumage. He goes on with his business high among the tall trees. It's a long way to Easter.

crystalline forces -
contracting

Rooks like black galaxies
above the fierce sunset.
A still winter night is coming;
for once the birds play raucous
in a windless world
spread flat against the flames
of day changing into dark.
The thousandfold flock
flows away to the tangled roost,
leaving us a shiver of frosty joy

Hive to Honeycomb

Imagine a candle,
alight like a river,
the same ever changing,
a star, a flower,
watch it passing,
falling into time,
its spirit released,
its beauty free,
a burning flower,
almost motionless,
a flower in winter,
moving in our thoughts,
lighting our minds.

In Spring will come the blossom,
but our hearts cannot blossom,
can they?

Imagine a candle
alight, like a river

molten sunlight

candle flame

The hives are sleeping

through storm and flood.

A warm day will wake them

to the golden crocus

but in winter this city sleeps.

Before, in autumn, the whole house

was sticky with the honey

from the heather on the hills.

What honey like the heather?

Thick, like jelly, the dark feel

of the windswept hills,

the gold of sunlit space untrodden.

You must cut the comb,

press it, strain it,

squeeze out the slow liquid,

and in so doing

see all that work destroyed,

the cells, the patient mathematics of the wax.

When Spring draws them to the Sun

they will form more,

bring the spirit nectar down to earth,

a holy work in an untidy house.

For now their wisdom lives in the flame

rising as fragrant as a prayer.

The Advent of a New Birth

Stand under the pungent firs,

catch one clear star through the branches.

For a moment be utterly silent,

lay down your load,

rest in the beginning.

Then you may hear Mary's song,

who comes with nothing

but her poverty,

humble as the earth is humble,

like a constant flame

not to be put out,

"Here I am,

I am the Lord's servant;

as you have spoken,

so be it."

The gift of light

we gratefully receive

But not for ourselves we would it achieve

We pass it on from one to the other

With glowing light

from sister to brother

Until all the world is flooded with light

Until all our hearts in love can unite

It will not be long ere

the darkness disappears

Christ draweth near.

(author unknown)

Advent is here, the garden made, the room

full of deep shadow and tender expectation.

This is the beginning in the dark of God's love.

In the darkened hall the child stands,

head held high, at the centre of the spiral.

Her forehead catches the light of the candle

she holds before her. She cups the apple, which

holds the candle, in her praying hands, her purpose

clear in her quiet eyes, in the sculpture of her brow. She

moves forward, as a dancer goes, surrendered to an inner

tune, on her way to set her Paradise candle down among the

sparkling shadows at her feet.

promise

Annunciation

expectancy

53

Kingdoms of Life

who could predict the progress of the plant?

    seed   root   green shoot   leaf   flower   seed

speechless and pure,

while we, we walk alone,

stumble and trample and blunder

and think we know it all.

spirits of fire, air, water, earth

A certain man descended from Jerusalem into Jericho, and fell into the hands
of thieves, who robbed him of his raiment and wounded him, and departed
leaving him half dead. And by chance there came a certain priest that
same way, and when he saw him he passed by. And likewise a Levite,
when he was come nigh to the place, went and looked on him, and passed by.

the spirits who form the roots
stand amazed at us,
we are so dull and blind,
our noses in the air or in our boots

Then a certain Samaritan, as he journeyed, came nigh
unto him, and when he saw him, had compassion on him

the spirits who lead the growing shoots
stir in us to do more than look -
to give each life its own true name,
to be devoted

and went to and bound up his wounds,
and poured in oil and wine, and
put him on his own beast, and brought him
to a common inn, and made provision for him.

the spirits who play on petal and on leaf
ask us not to be stuck -
to breathe, to touch,
to love the light and dark

And on the morrow when he departed,
he took out two pence and gave them to the host
and said to him. Take care of him,
and whatsoever thou spendest more,
when I come again, I will recompense thee.

the spirits who prepare the seeds
thunder to encourage us
to be large, to reach out
to life's demands

the world's noise
shuts out these voices
but unless we listen
we will not be at peace

(from the Gospel of Luke Chapter 10, William Tyndale, 1534)

Painting the Rainbow Bridge

We are in a master painter's workshop six hundred years ago. The apprentice grinds the pigments - lapis lazuli, verdigris, cinnabar. From mussel and crocus too, the earth is gathered and crushed to give new beauty. On the wall is a portrait of Saint Luke, the patron, the master painter, in the act of painting Mary from life. His eyes are on her, wonderfully calm and attentive. Luke was a doctor. He is the one who tells us of this Christmas night of angels and shepherds, of the child born into the chill night and laid in the hay, the warm breath of beasts upon him. For a doctor is an artist, following the heart, unearthing the soul's rainbow, and a painter is a physician, searching faces, witnessing the weather of lives.
This night let Luke be with us, giving body to this birth, mixing the colours of love.

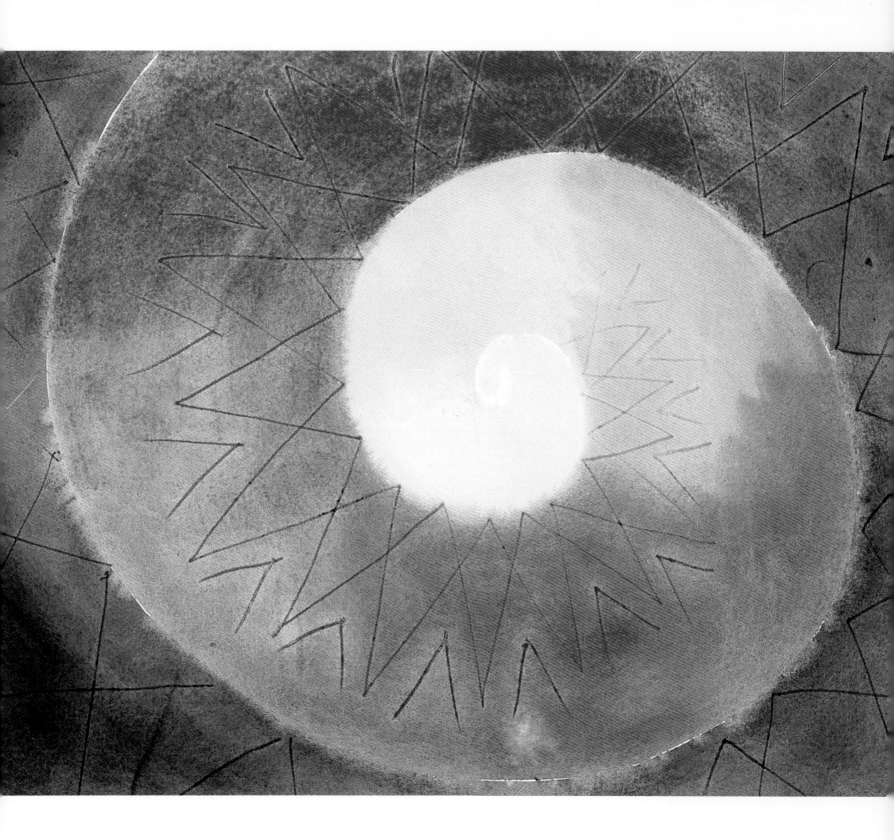

Holy Nights

It is now stark mid-winter. There is a pause in earth's cosmic breathing.

When a new-born child comes into a house, a special magic is felt where past and future gather into a timeless present. So it is, at Christmas, on Earth.

We all long for a time to stop, a time to be still, something more than a simple break from work. The traditional holiday period of the Holy Nights - from Christmas Eve to Epiphany (or Three Kings Day) on the sixth of January - remains, today, a period of renewal, a 'time out of time', an interval during which we can receive new inspiration and strength.

In our journey we meet the joyful power of music and music-making to take us out of our ordinary selves. Meanwhile, a New Year has begun. By Epiphany we can emerge from our dream-time with fresh spark and resolve.

Christmas Eve

I saw a sweet and simple sight,

A blissful bride, a blossom bright

That morning made and mirth arising

A maiden mother meek and mild

In cradle kept a newborn child

That softly slept, she sat and sang

Lullay, lullow, lully, lully, lully,

Lully, lully, lully, lully,

Lullow, lully, lully, baw, baw,

My bairn, sleep softly now

(fifteenth century)

It is a rose,
a newborn rose,
longed for, hoped for,
a wave breaking
open, this soft
whorl of flame, this
whirlpool of love.

Christmas Eve, the tree is dressed for Celebration but under the glory, the glinting, breathe in the green shade, the scent of something ancient and patient. The old father waits for the birth of the child and all that labour will bring to the needy earth.

there is light when we admit our fears
and our need to deny

At the turning point of Time,

The Spirit Light of the World

Entered the stream of Earthly Evolution.

Darkness of Night

Had held its sway;

Day-radiant Light

there is light when we struggle and shout
and laugh at our helplessness

there is light when we give and take
and know each other

Poured into the souls of men:

Light that gives warmth

To simple shepherds' hearts,

Light that enlightens

there is light when there is
only my light in the great dark

The wise heads of kings.

there is light when I have hope
to go on into the unknown

O Light Divine!

O Sun of Christ!

Warm Thou our hearts,

Enlighten Thou our heads,

That good may become

What from our hearts we would found

And from our heads direct

With single purpose.

RS

Birth of the Light

Come, Child, into our hearts and still the storm

Made by our selfish wishes wrestling there;

And weave again the fabric of mankind

Out of Thy Light, Thy Life, Thy Loving Fire.

AB

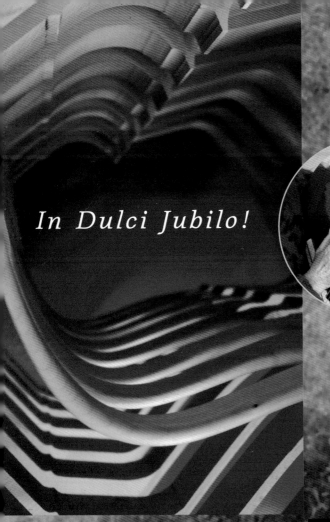

In Dulci Jubilo!

He worked all night to make it.

Shaping the wood to a heart,

stretching the strings clear across;

returning, giving us back

this instrument for love's hands.

He held it by his heart beat,

he pressed the string, set it free,

let his soul sing on the sea,

alert and quiet, near, far,

and the tone sought other hearts

warming the air of the morn.

(In celebration of the first modern lyre made in 1926.)

At Christmas we went with friends to sing carols in the High Street, rattling our tins, for missionaries, I think. The best was always Good King Wenceslas - my father sang the King, solo, and I sang the page. Loud and clear the song passed between us among the faces in the dark.

I remember my mother singing
  and the moon so thin and curly;
   they are one, song and moon above
and my head against her breast
    rising and falling with the soft song.

melody

harmony

rhythm

beat

He held the bell in his hand. The music tipped and danced from end to end of the line of ringers, each with a bell

poised to bring one tone to the tune's flow with the firm swing of an arm, the strike of tongue on metal's bright curve.

Still he held his bell mute. The smallest bell, the highest bell.

In rehearsals he had been tense, waiting for the right moment with tight wrist, anticipating; but now he was in the swing,

the rhythm caressing his soul, loving the shape and space of the melody, the harmony.

And then it came, the firm struck tone placed on the beat of his heart, at one with them all.

Here it comes again, the music is returning, yes, the arm swings true... keeping time beautiful

Time Out of Time

time

shines · burns · turns · upside down · reminds · dreams · returns · hides · bursts · prays · waits · inscribes · calls · binds

glowing embers
smoke rising thin

dumb beasts succour
a sleeping child

bare trees stand black
by Easter's road

ice in fragments
asks for loving

windswept reed bed
this year, ever

hard seed splitting
under bare fields

song, rhythm, joy
fly from our hearts

long calm pure dark
so close to light

sun inside us
through winter blast

best of men, worst
survive, destroyed

bells toll days pass
both dawn and dusk

sifting debris
for signs of life

flapping sails tug
tide on the turn

Melchior gold

We are not Kings, stern Queens,
we are not magicians, not wise,
but we have had dreams,
been given intimations
of strange journeys
which we must find the strength to make,
had hints of gifts
to bring to some deciphered birth,
have seen amid the myriad
one plain star that stands there for me.

Balthazar frankinsence

Caspar myrrh

The Gifts of Epiphany

We have met here by the river side;
we have brought all our baggage;
now we can cross, go on together,
wade the cold water and then - who knows -
bright banners flapping in the wind,
a leopard on a golden chain,
strange birds in cages speaking strange words -
I am overwhelmed by all this
light. I need help, a friend.
I hear echoes of deeds done long past,
thunder rumbles from the life to come,
I stand at the edge, so thin,
like ice cracking to let eternity in.
I am ready for adventure
but there are secrets we must share,
going together. Come, in we plunge.

Crafts of the Earth

Winter is at its hardest and coldest, the Earth withdrawn, with the crystalline-forming forces at their strongest. But the light of the sun grows gently brighter. While, outwardly, all remains cold and dormant, soon the sap will rise and the seed will germinate, as the warmth and light penetrate the cold and dark. The buds on the trees and the birds' bright plumage signal that the natural world is preparing for Spring.

Candlemas comes on the second day of February, forty days after Christmas. This festival celebrates the recognition, by the elderly Simeon and Anna, of the fulfilment of the prophesy of the coming of the Christ Child, as told in Luke's Gospel.

It is a good time to confirm the covenant between humankind and the forces of nature. The season of candles is completed by the making and lighting of a candle in the earth itself - placing warmth and light within the still cold soil as an expression of gratitude, co-operation and commitment.

It reminds us that care for the land is so much needed. All beings depend on it. The seeds sprout, grow and are in turn consumed by humans and animals. This cycle of nourishment from plant to humans needs constant vigilance and care if the delicate balance is to remain healthy.

In our journey, we turn to the crafts of the land such as pottery and basketwork. Clay and willow, the mineral and the plant, are worked to fashion bowls and baskets - ready to receive the fruit of the forthcoming harvest.

Candlemas

The ice on the window pane is silent,

crystal has built upon crystal, finished,

a perfect simulacrum of a fern.

I can see nothing through its pure beauty.

We must make things supple,

swim in the imagination of change.

We have made a promise to the Earth -

To stay alive, to have hope.

The ice melts - my breath -

I see a man stark against the white outside.

He is walking my way

across the jagged cracks.

we kneel and place

the light into the soil

acknowledging our

dependency

yet willing to be

co-workers with the

Earth which is the

Body of Christ

When Rembrandt died, poor and lonely, in 1669, he was working on a painting of Simeon holding Jesus on this day of Candlemas, the child a precious light cradled in the old man's arms.

Seeds

Seeds are our survival,
these tiny glistening grains,
knobbles, flakes, dust, fluff -
cupped in the palm of my hand.
They grow weak today, chemical,
deformed to dull machines
making no mistakes;
when they should be as bright
as the scattered stars,
strong and surprising.
So save them, stir them,
even sing to your seeds,
for seeds are our survival.

Do trees have seeds?
How strange. Chestnuts, yes, but seeds?
They are so big, trees, and seeds are so small.
Do they really need seeds?

It was a pine tree above the sea. In France. I passed it every day, solid, knotted, on the cliff edge, looking down on the sea. I climbed and tugged free some stone hard cones and brought them home. They sat on a window sill till the next summer's sun cracked them open and freed the seeds. I sowed them and up the tasselled seedlings came, surprised to be in Scotland, shivering in the cold winds and searching for the sun. They have kept going, established themselves, thrived. They seem settled, if bemused, wondering why no-one walks by nibbling a baguette.

Earth Care

the animals go about
unminding; see their tracks
criss-cross in the snow, a pause
to sniff or make their mark.
We are different. We have a
knowing, a mistrust that can
leave us full of fear, desperate
to make ourselves a cage.
But, thank God, life is in us,
and love - just on to the next
crest to see down into the
valley, just ask one more gentle
question so you can speak, just
one more spadeful of shining
soil. And when we do, our love
is answered by a greater love.

We leave the cage behind, we
find faith, and then we can
move mountains.

In winter he goes quiet.
He's a gardener, you see,
a very quiet man,
in winter time.
When the ground freezes
he goes to earth, silent.
Not morose, or rude, or sleepy,
just very, very quiet.
It can be unnerving.
He speaks, smiles, replies
but inside there's something
turning, moving.
He's working on something
slowly in his warm mind
as he walks the iron-hard field,
or sits, lost in the sinuous flames.

*earth
and man -
a mutual
fragility*

From furrows dark in light-filled air

Green leaves growing

In all we eat from light we feed

Ripened in sun's glowing

The fruits of earth to live we need

Gratitude showing.

CAL

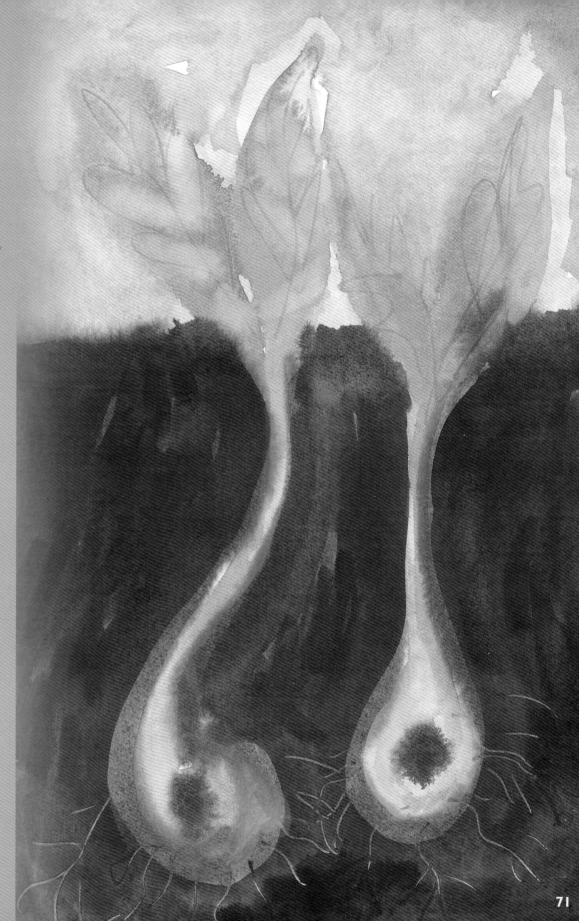

Brother Animal

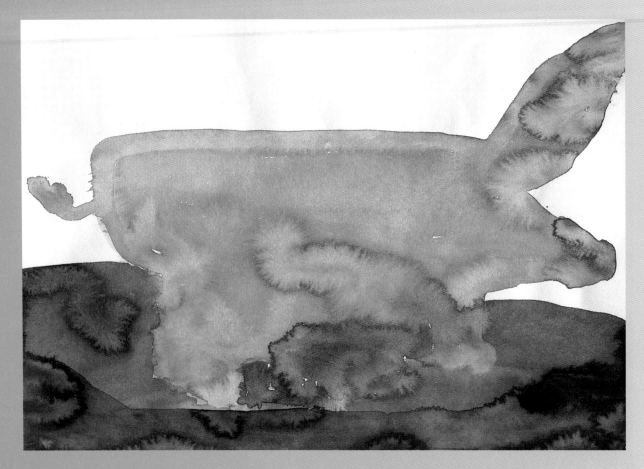

A still night, only the moon moves and the starry creatures of the sky,

each constellation telling a story of sacrifice for earth's life and ours -

Lion, Bull, Whale, even a pale Giraffe.

    In the house the mother is asleep but her soul hovers near, her

ears are open for the new-born child who has come into this

house and who sleeps in the cradle, his sleep among the stars

and the warm creatures who move through his dreams.

This time is theirs, the dark hours of stillness.

in the kitchen the mouse opens
wide his beady black eyes,
frightened he has left himself behind.

in the field the tiny harvest mouse
has woven a womb
for her naked young.

down in the cellar
the rats are restless,
long tails slide with menace.

by the fire the old dog sleeps,
his nose explores,
he whimpers for the long-lost hunt.

the cat is poised,
her tail tip flicks,
she is after blood.

In the Heart - the loom of Feeling,

In the Head - the light of Thinking,

In the Limbs - the strength of Will,

Weaving of radiant Light,

Strength of the Weaving

Light of the surging Strength:

Lo, this is Man!

RS

the cows chew dreams,
fermenting deep within
a universe of food.

the sheep lie peaceful,
their needs are few,
voices softly longing for the hills.

the bear lies curled,
clumsy, a big baby,
growing fat for winter.

the leopard is the night,
her skin alive,
muscles through the moonlight.

the porcupine digs,
heavy and repellent
he hides himself away.

the round seal strains,
slips into the sea,
a curve of darker grace.

the tiger is abroad
swimming the swirling river
ready for life and death.

Work my hands

Strong and warm

Work to make

A lively form

Push and press

And squeeze and roll

Work to make

A form that's whole.

(author unknown)

you - the potter and the pot

one - the hollow of the clay, the hand

blind - the mud, the man who shapes,

attentive to the tone,

deep down the circling tone,

the whispered song stirring the sticky earth.

The potter watches the clay

rising from the silent spinning wheel,

a jar for water and for wine.

Eyes intent, elbow bent,

he is a patient man,

enduring, unassuming,

but see him as a priest

lifting up the calm clay

in the thinking of his fingers,

curving the contradictions into one...

Forming the Vessel

this pot, this plate

the same everyday

but each one living

like a new leaf.

he takes the clay,

the silent lump

and turns God's working

on the wheel of the world.

this bowl, this cup,

bulky, soon broken,

has come from the beauty

in his listening mind.

Pottery

In India I remember the piles, so precarious, but none toppled, of new household pots - plain, warm, brown. Made for the Harvest Festival, a time to buy new vessels for the year ahead. But in a quiet grove, a holy place, outside the village, a gathering of clay animals to call or thank a god - tigers, horses, oxen - some new and brightly painted, some faded, broken, going back to earth. A heap of man's trust in God and in the breath of life.

bowl   *vase*   *cup*   *plate*

Bending the Willow

Against the dark grained planks of the shed wall
the bolts of willow rods stand upright,
bundled,
ordered,
chestnut and ivory, dried apricot,
ready to be bent.

a shelter

Each rod is a journey,
as tall as a man,
thinning from butt to tip,
each with a curve, a belly;
its form a motion of the sun
caught in matter.

a hurdle

All I need is a wall to lean against,
a floor, a board, a knife, a bodkin.
Then it's just hand and eye
and the growing basket
between my knees
and the weight inside to settle the space.

a basket

I will fashion a soft shelter,
a cradle for apples or eggs,
for a dog to turn and lie in,
or even for my head - yes -
a rush hat with ribbons hanging,
to go dancing on the green.

a cradle

I sat quiet in the sun,
wove clematis, periwinkle,
rose, bramble - vines and strands,
to make a hedgerow basket;
and to and fro the chaffinch went
sharing nest stuff from the pile.

BASKETRY

Willow sway   wind sweep the willing sticks

willow bend   light weave the winter holt

willow bow   now cut the supple rods.

The Spring of New Life

 The first tentative touches of Spring. Snowdrops. Cherry blossom.

We understand, though, how vulnerable is this fresh beauty to the last of winter wind and frost.

In southern lands, autumn is coming, bringing its storms. The equinox is reached, creating another moment of balance as, once again, day equals night. We feel both joy and hardship, weariness and new life.

Those mixed emotions mirror our confusions concerning illness and healing. We sometimes hope for a life without suffering, yet cherish the love and wisdom that often come through meeting loss or crisis. Such contradictions!

Through the art of drama we meet both our weaknesses and our strengths, the failings and virtues we find in ourselves and others. We learn to cope with contradiction. Carnival, with its costumes and masks, comedy and tragedy working together, shows the interplay of good and evil and helps to prepare the soul for Lent.

In the festivals of Holy Week and Easter, we celebrate the culminating events of Christ's earthly life. We remember the mystery of death and resurrection of the great Easter drama performed on earth's stage.

On this part of the journey, in this mood of struggle and overcoming, healing in its wider sense may be found. Therapies, though practised throughout the year as an art, have their own space at Eastertide, as do bread-making and the healing properties of herb growing and preparation.

What we offer in devotion to others heals us as well. Our small acts of love are the inner complement to the Spring time of joyful rejuvenation.

Reawakening Earth

Sun and squall sweep across the hillside, clearing away the old year's tangles, leaving it clean and dazzling. The fast stream is full with Winter's snow and new Spring's growing light.

A dipper bobs on a smooth stone, plump and black with a quick dab of white; the slim wagtail's stops and dashes are lost against the din and the mottled rocks.

A heron stands motionless in a pool that catches the blue, and then the grey of the stinging sleet. This is their home through the year but it is Spring and time for the bright-eyed salmon to be gone.

The big fish, the kelts, spent from mating, are going back to the sea, their long climb to the light done, the glowing colours of Autumn now fading on their bellies. They came here faithful to the winter sun; to look up, like the glinting pools, to the stars - to drink in light and take it down to us, for the earth's life.

In the end down to the dark salt sea go the old ones, taking bright motion into the soup of oceans. The multitudes of the young smolt go now. They have lived their years here in the cold clear hills. They are getting ready for the sea. They go, as Spring goes, to seek substance, to feed and grow fat. They will, years hence, themselves return, climb from the estuary to this stirred stream to receive the light. Now they go down, sunbeams in the cold flowing.

blossom bursting

leaves unfurling

stems shooting

roots quickening

Along the spiny blackthorn branch
blossom spreads, the juice of Spring
hanging on the liquid air.
Our hands, yours and mine, reach out,
loosened from paralysis,
touching across the abyss.

The King's Jester

Winter puppet show. The children sit in the dark and watch the lighted space where stories pass and colours glow. The tiny stage grows wide. Here are feelings as old as dreams; scraps of cloth alive with what lives deep down in us, innocent; letting them see evil and see faith, letting them sense how God's spirit lives in each of us as we go about in our scattered selves.

Each day a play,

a game not trivial

but blessed - forgiveness its essence.

We must start anew,

laugh, weep, be lost, and found,

let people come to us, us feel,

let the drama of the day be done

and then at the end

after the fun, cries, disguises,

enter the silence,

all offence forgotten.

a moment for Shakespeare and his Globe

From high above the trumpeter summons the latecomers.

The bold flag ripples with the sign of Hercules holding the round

world on his shoulders.

This theatre a daylight crowded world. Just a scribbled book,

a quick practice at the battle. Where did the magic come from?

Acts of discovery and love. Moulding hearts, working the imagination

alive in a circle, a noisy globe of moved minds.

"for 'tis your thoughts that now must deck our Kings."

Forward she came

and her eyes were starlight

and the hard mask was gone:

the princess now,

and we her courtiers

giving rightful homage.

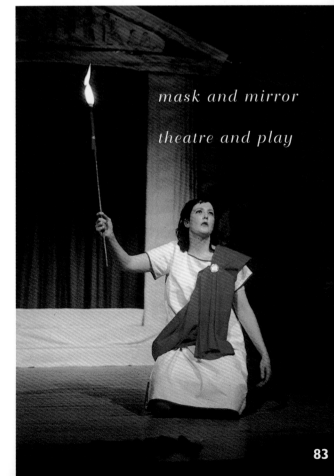

mask and mirror

theatre and play

Passion Week

What will become of this holy week?
It is like looking at a child and asking
What will become of her as she grows,
as each day becomes the next.

Sacrament, moment of waking,
act of mystery, resonant,
like a long-wingéd bird
skimming the deep sea swell.

Sunday

the child cries
coming to the house of the soul,
"my home is elsewhere
but this earth is my place of work."

baptism

Monday
the young one
hides a secret inside,
"I must find my own way
towards my death. Who will help?"

confirmation

Tuesday
when I speak, and take in speech
I change myself;
the meaning of things
I carry as I go.

consultation

Wednesday

a time of recognition,
welcoming the bitter and the sweet.
The circle is unbroken
of the seen and the unseen.

marriage

Thursday
this one day is every day;
the need for bread,
to be made new,
to walk with Christ.

communion

Friday
may I be given grace,
to have a voice, to bless,
but not my voice alone
for then it is not grace.

ordination

Saturday
a time to gather in,
to press juice from the fruit,
"I will live again,
I will live better."

annointing

Until today Adam's race has had its head in a bag, seeing seasons come and go, the trance of Winter, the restless Sun and Moon, the rising life of Spring, the rivers going on and on, but all with no shape, no story. Now Christ has risen and we can see that all the natural world is gathered up in the body in which Christ rose, that is in the body of each one of us.

there is the matter
of wind and air　　　*that makes our body breathe*

there is the matter
of heat and fire　　　*that makes our red blood warm in our bodies*

there is the matter
of the sun and stars　　*that makes the light in our eyes*

there is the matter
of bitterness and salt　*that makes tears and anger in our hearts*

there is the matter
of stones and clay　　*that makes the flesh and bones of our limbs*

there is the matter
of flowers and
colours of the earth　*that makes the complexion of our faces*

All of the world arose with him. Today we are set free from a dark house. We have known God as we slept. Today we wake to Christ.

(Adapted extracts from 'The Evernew Tongue Here Below' - an Irish poem of a thousand years ago.)

Breaking the Bread

From where do we get our bread?

Not from my wise head.

We can do nothing to make it come,

however hard the work we've done.

However much we toil and grieve,

we wait, we receive.

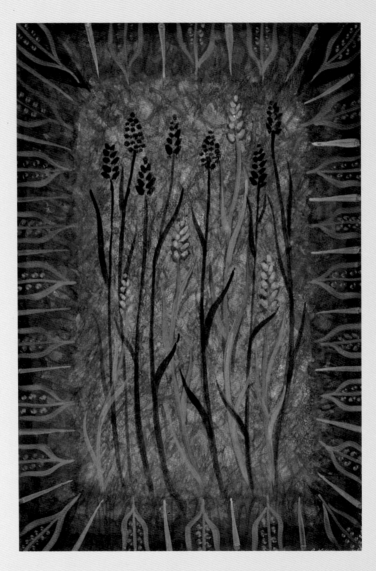

Nervous of fungus?

made numb by fungi?

obnoxious, poisonous,

toadstools and mould,

smuts and rusts

you can't control.

Then, please, remember yeasts

and lichen and tiny fine hairs on roots.

These are fungi, guiding life,

keeping earth clean,

bubbling in bowels of earth and us,

budding and growing,

making beer brew and cheese ripen,

letting the fresh flour spring and rise.

one oven for the village, by the church, in the square, to which the people were called once a week when the fierce fire had burnt down and the ash scraped clear. Then the women came with loaves on trays, some shaped, some simple, ready for the clean heat. And while the fat loaves baked, the women talked the week till it had a shape and a crust and the children watched the light glint on polished knives, ready to cut the first hot slices.

I'm the first one awake in the village, the first, before the cowman or the storeman, the driver or the priest. The first one out under the stars. I like to be alone with the stars of the morning as I walk to the

bakery. They're still there as I weigh out the flour and the sound of the scales falling and the dough thumping on the table echoes in the empty dark. It's silence till the jobs are done, the light has come and it's time to drink coffee and see faces. I like to think of work days beginning in Winter. I like to think of the smell of the ovens spreading over the village in Spring, people stopping to breathe in the day's bread beneath blue skies. Each day the rising of the bread, the light down in the dough bubbling up to the sun. I like to be home before dark, just as the evening star is telling me already of tomorrow's mystery.

kneading

moulding

waiting

rising

this child is bent in body,

he lives an outcast,

naked and wild.

I have clothes ready to cover him.

this child is weak and restless,

she falls, she stumbles,

she cannot find the way.

I will offer bread to strengthen her.

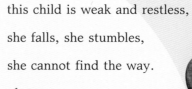

this child is scared out of her wits,

the storm is tossing her,

the dreams are drowning.

I will stay awake to comfort her.

this child is blind,

he sits begging at the roadside,

he will not lift his head.

I will bend down to help him stand.

September 5th - *There were several butterflies in the room today, looking for a place to shelter for the winter. John was watching them but he didn't want me to see his interest. We had a silent game, him struggling with his wish to look, the light coming and going in his deep dark eyes.*

October 14th - *We went for a walk in the woods today, crisp and beautiful. John dragged his feet and I went at his pace, painfully slow. He was waiting for me to say something, get annoyed. We came upon a deer, a hind. For some reason she ignored us although she was in the open. We watched her in the slanting sun, quite plain, grey, but such utter grace. John held my hand as we watched. Suddenly she was gone, leaping through the autumn air.*

November 12th - *I really lost my temper today. John was so careless and clumsy, spilling paint and expecting everything to revolve around him. I came home to a cold and empty house and a plate of over-cooked spaghetti, feeling very sorry for myself. I could see John smiling.*

December 8th - *We painted a picture of a fir tree with candles. Everything went right. John kept lifting his brush and head and looking, I don't know where, like a conductor looking over an orchestra, and then back to the paper where the colours flowed soft and bright. At the end he went over to the window and stood looking out at the frosty world, lost in... something.*

The Herb Garden

I found the old herb garden by chance; it was almost lost in the scrub of hazel and elder and holly. But there were too many snowdrops and they seemed to have been placed, planned. It must have been cultivated once. Under the ivy and honeysuckle I found the crumbling walls. It had been a circle, maybe twelve paces across, a low wall, a sign not a barrier. Inside the circle there were remnants of hedges; leathery, peppery box still marking the edges of the cross-shaped path that divided the circle in four. I found the centre that first day and turned to follow round the compass of the crumbling wall that kept the space intact. Was I the only one alive who had seen this garden? I found old clumps of lovage and horseradish just sending up new growth, lines of rue and straggly sage and lavender, clumps of feverfew fresh green. The old plants had survived through all the years when they had been needed for weddings and funerals. Other healing plants had been drawn to this enclosure from the woods and hedges - they came as summer came - valerian and meadowsweet and borage, and all around, like a sky full of stars, yarrow light and loving. I have cleared the garden, tidied it, but not too much. I have planted lemon balm for the bees (and for my gloomy days). They love to come and go across the walls and so do I. It is a place where I may rest.

Heart Listening

In the harsh wilderness of Arabia

the thorny shrub stands gaunt against the rocks.

Resin drips from the cut stem,

thick and aromatic,

green, growing brown as it hardens.

Such strong fragrance in the sharp shadowed desert.

Gather this myrrh, this balm,

carry it from the east.

It is the third gift for the Christ child

after the splendour of gold and frankincense,

a gift most human, and weighted with God.

It is for healing,

it is for dying and for going through.

Nature is not distant,
out there, beyond us.
We are entwined;
but we have eyes,
and we make mirrors,
and see our bodies
broken from our souls.
Let them join, let them part,
let life come and go
not bound to weary death,
but keeping us
just brave, just vulnerable,
catching blessings
from the humdrum day.

priest

doctor

nurse

therapist

The doctor is with her patient. She is listening - the pain is here, and here; the moods - despair and hope, and resignation, come and go. It's hard to find the cause. The patient is waiting for the right medicine, for healing. In the doctor's room are books and implements, knowledge and skill. There are others there in spirit as they talk - the nurse who has touched, the therapist who has listened to the breath, the priest who has helped the story to be told. The doctor is a teacher. She has her eyes and voice but there is also the angel who is among them, the angel their common work has summoned. Together they find a meaning in what seems just a foreign thing. Plant and mineral and human help make this room a world: an act of substance and of love.

flavours   scents   ointments   balms   medicines

A Circle of Flames

The sun is climbing back towards its zenith. May bursts upon us with nature's abundance and beauty. We can feel the forces of new growth and life, now at their strongest, all around - just look at the trees, the wheat, the new-born animals, the flowers colouring the landscape. The air itself feels alive, from the glory of the dawn chorus to the swirling clouds of early summer. We are reminded of the image of the *Dove*.

So we approach our journey's end with our gaze drawn upwards, one cycle of our spiral almost complete. Yet a vital step remains before we return to mid-summer. Our enthusiasm - our *Flame* - is fired partly by this season, much by the mood of the time. It is Ascension, when Christ unites with the realms of life around our earth and, in our souls, intuitions of new ways of working can arise, more dynamic yet also more sensitive.

The period between Ascension and Whitsun can also be a time of withdrawal and reflection, as experienced by the first Christians, but awakens the conviction that great individual and social changes are 'in the air'. Whitsun itself brings the opportunity for confident, loving responsibility, the time to recognise and respond to the *Flame* of others, to work together in community, a 'Whitsun' community, in a circle, a circle of *Flames*.

On this last step of our journey, we witness the great medieval story of Parsival, whose path of self-discovery gives us wonderful insights into the human being's quest for inner growth. The power of harmony between individual and group in an artistic form is reflected in the new art of movement - Eurythmy. Similar creative powers are needed in the very process of community-building, the last, perhaps most challenging and mysterious art of our journey, which we call the 'Social Art', and which will take us far into the future.

Clouds Ascending

drifting

A warm May morning, the sky alive with bird song

and growing cloud. The hillside is still damp, mossy. The child lies on her *moving*

tummy, absorbed. On a flat rock she has gathered things - the two halves of an eggshell

the colour of heaven, a handful of dandelions dying and soft, a rock with crystals glinting, cones

and stones, shells and bog cotton. She places her pink scarf round her treasures like a snaking wall.

Above her the clouds are huge moving hills. Sun and shade run, shaping the land, mound and hollow, like the

potter's hand. The quick breeze strokes the heads of the thin-stalked grass and stirs the still pond's pictured

world awake, mixing heaven and earth below the rising mountains of the sky. All this is in the child although she

does not look up, does not inspect. Her soul has eyes, she lives with angels in her thoughts. She is with the being

of the clouds but does not name him yet. This day will live in her when hard things come: anger and apathy,

eyes grown cold or will not open. She will find the day of clouds again, feel the bounty, the love

surrounding her small body. She sings to her things on the flat rock. The things reply - the stones, the

shells, the whispering clouds and the sky. They say something she has heard before, in

heaven, in her heart, in the light playing on her mother's face. The clouds go

silent over her, holding the burgeoning of the comforting earth.

changing

transforming

Eurythmy - Limbs that Sing

she runs alone across the sand
    like a gathering wave about to break

he climbs the sheer smooth rock face
    light as birdsong

he bears the pilgrim through the river's surge
    his steps as true as promises

she strokes her daughter's desolate face
    her hand as holy as a rainbow

movements of grace and desire
    recalling timeless beauty to our eyes

I seek within

The working of creative forces,

The life of creative powers.

Earth's gravity is telling me

Through the word of my feet,

Air's wafting forms are telling me

Through the singing of my hands,

And Heaven's light is telling me

Through the thinking of my head,

How the great World in Man

Speaks, sings and thinks.

RS

I want the sounds I utter, the words,

the bearing of my limbs, to matter.

I long to take part, to create,

enable words, hands, to animate.

The pure dove, the butterfly,

these I cannot make, but I can shape

the air they touch, can lead the flow into speech,

can carry space as I go,

offering my muscles to the generous sun,

my dance to the measure of the stars.

sculpting the air

A Festival of Flowers

from the maypole's high
top spreads the circle of
ribbons to the dancers
poised below to plait the
path of friendship. Colours
will cross, above, below,
knitting each into kinship
under the tent of heaven.

In the dance my love I seek
honouring and setting
in the dance myself I meet
siding now and arming
bow and curtsy, right and left,
my love, now will I find you?
changing places, linking arms
with a kiss my heart will bind you.

On the village green one old oak,
strange, huge, with sharp pointed
bony limbs antlered against the sky.
Do not think it dead or dying -
its life comes and goes,
a new crown is forming,
roots are finding new holds and flows.
It lives its history,
its dead bits visited with life
indomitable.
It is right that here they come to dance,
beneath this antique thing
worthy to welcome back the Spring.

the mother to the baby speaks
    it is like the beating of her heart,
    it lets the baby rest, her journey done

the mother to the child speaks
    attentive to the young one's question,
    to the wisdom that she brings

the father to the child speaks
    not denying the dark,
    pointing to the light

the old man to the young woman speaks
    mostly he tells old stories
    and then a gentle silence

the young man to the grandmother speaks
    he has a fear he must share,
    he dares to release the words

the wife to the husband speaks
    she offers confirmation
    to untwist the knot

the husband to the wife speaks
    he tries to tell her
    how bright the candle of her soul

the old man to the young man speaks
    it is time to get going,
    no more hiding, or denying

the child to the grandmother speaks
    hoping that they share
    the same secrets

the mother to the young man speaks
    asking him to forget the hurt,
    asking him not to wound

the young man to the mother speaks
    telling her to take away her arms
    and let his flame be free

the old woman to her husband speaks
    accepting what they missed,
    giving thanks for truth

Whitsun Flame

This Whitsunday they can all come out
of the house, go alone and go together,
carrying the word each needs to speak,
each needs to hear. They share their fortunes,
undoing time's divisions.

imagine a community

An Inner Path

To us it is given

At no stage ever to rest.

They live and they strive the active

Human beings from life unto life

As plants grow from springtime

To springtime - ever aloft,

Through error upward to truth,

Through fetters upward to freedom,

Through illness and death

Upward to beauty, to health and life.

RS

No longer children,
our learning starts with loss,
something stuck or dull.
There was something once, warm,
but it has gone.

I am lost   *Parzival wanders*
I am cursed
I saw visions
but they passed
I have no name
no name and no home
I am alone
a ghost who is lost.

Then comes suffering, a spur, some
determination to go on, some longing.

All whom I love I must leave   *Parzival is ashamed*
my heart is made
just to grieve
I go from this place
in disgrace
I weave my way
with nothing to believe:
a leaf shaking on a tree.

Last comes interest, facing beauty and
the beast, the working of the word.

Parzival struggles

No more travelling in shadows
heavy hearted, humming a sad song.
Something has been saved,
a tough seed,
a speck of gold.
My soul opens, a bud unfolding,
not bound to the old,
awake and slowly wise.

Grail, cup of shining love,
pure flower passed through fire,
bowl open to the strength of stars,
we seek you in our fleeting house,
to bind us and to make us kind.

Parzival at last asks

"What is wrong?"
"Why do you suffer?"
"Why are you weak?"
Sometimes answers, sometimes
silence too full for talk,
but asking is enough,
enough to begin with.
I'll not disown your troubles.
I lift the cup of love.

To wonder at beauty,
Stand guard over truth,
Look up to the noble,
Resolve on the good.
This leadeth man truly
To purpose in living,
To right in his doing,
To peace in his feeling,
To light in his thinking.
And teaches him trust,
In the working of God,
In all that there is,
In the width of the world,
In the depth of the soul.

RS

The end of a long summer's day. They sit at the table, where nasturtiums spill and flow from the vase, red and yellow against a vivid green of active peace. Pat has been weeding, row after row, hour after hour, lonely work. Her back aches from all those hours upside down.

The children are asleep. She wishes she had not been so cross at bed time. Inflexible, like the rows, the hoe with its sweat-stained, smooth handle. She sees again the butterfly lost in its impossible dance from flower to flower, as unpredictable as love.

hoe   *spade*   *rake*

Will has been making hay. His eyes and throat are raw, his neck aches from turning back and forth. His head is full of engine. Why did he keep remembering that hurt done to him? The unkind word of a friend which he had let take root in his soul. Turning it over in the turning engine.

Suddenly he smells the hay as it will be in winter, the quiet barn, the crunch of cattle chewing sweet hay. The colours of sunset fade. Cows call in the cool of night. They look at each other across the flame, too tired to talk of love. Their hands, grained and used, reach out to meet by the tumbling flowers.

fork *plough* *harrow*

Corpus Christi

Perhaps we can convince ourselves

that the moon is perfect,

a pale wafer,

round and faceless,

but not the Earth;

the Earth is a mess of beauty

(endless the shoreline, vast the lustrous sea),

and full of faces, loved ones -

in the blush of colour on your cheek

sensing heaven's pulse.

heals bread alive makes paths carry trust breath above shine earth truth

Christos

Recall the street, the block, of sixty or a hundred years ago. Brooklyn or Bethnal Green. A poor neighbourhood, a place, perhaps, from which your family came. The mother at the hub, the one who brought children into the world, and then was there to help her daughters when their time came; who moved, tired, between wet washing and tear-stained faces. When she went to the shops she knew every face. Her house an open door for the family to call and when she died her memory kept them together. Fathers worked and drank beer slowly and hoped, or half hoped, their sons might not have to labour with their hands. A place with living history, a common territory, with people connected, and valued because connected. Family, bonds of blood. You turned down your street and found your life. Ancient ties now pressed into cities.

Today we are mixed. We drift. We must make efforts. We are no longer meant to live with kin or even seek like-minded friends for shelter. We must try small ways of living with strangers - tentative, trusting, asking. No more belief in brick-built security, but having faith in the one with whom we act. Throw away that sad stiff mask and let your face be free. Then see if we can fit the broken half I've kept safe in my pocket; see if we can work it in with the piece you shyly trust to show me you have saved. The bits may not belong together, may not quite fit, but we'll work at it.

The healthy social life is found
When in the mirror of each human soul
The whole community finds its reflection
And when in the Community
The virtue of each one is living.

RS

The Tune of the Year is Myself!

I can be good when I want to be
But I can be bold when I want to be

Sometimes I can be funny
and sometimes I can't.
In the back of my mind there's my birthday.

I feel cold because I'm so tiny.
The essence of my life is weaving cushions.

In summer I'm quite well,
every season I try to take notice of people.

The nightmares I have coming
like summer and winter,
first there's a warm expression
then there's coldness again.

The tune of the year is myself.

MT

I Dunno

I am happy and great, tall;
it's difficult what you want to do.

My hair and face is special.
I'm happy when I get up in the morning,
and I work hard.

I eat my breakfast,
sometimes oats, sometimes porridge.
I think of myself, think of what I'm doing.

I walk - sometimes to the beach,
sometimes to Ballymoney.

JB

Path of The Sun

The sun's northward reach is almost done,

earth's light has left to find

an answer from the vanished stars.

We are invited to eternity.

So then I went walking in the short night,

to go above, to be at the mountain top

when the sun came back so early to my earth,

to climb, head bent to the slope, lost

in footstep and breath; stride and breathe

in a rhythm that ended thinking. I was there

and felt blessed and less and more than human

when that consuming sun overcame my face

and freedom made me blind with bliss.

I came down through rain

that hung and sun that speared the mist.

That rough path had glittering rivulets

dividing and combining before my feet,

the air swaying with rainbows.

I saw shapes below me - wagons, horses,

men, women, children, on the move,

a tinker family taking the high pass.

I stopped, afraid of strangers, stood aside,

and they passed me, not trusting to my eye,

simple and proud they passed,

deliberate, absent, a whistle to a dog,

and left me looking for my home.

As I looked down into the valley
I saw them so small, taking in the hay
under dark clouds rolling from the South.
I joined my friends in the field,
lifting the green bales high with long forks
urgent to build the slow swaying load -
hot purpose of sweat and tight tendons -
to save the hay before the spoiling flood.
The last cart rocked down the rutted track
as the first vast drops fell
on our raw faces and raw hands.
The black air broke open with labour's end
and let heaven wash clear this dusty world.

Epilogue

Since our journey began on that Sunday in 1927, with the candles that were eventually to light the flame of Camphill, the Movement has grown to over a hundred centres world-wide. Each community has chosen where to place its candle in a spiral of ever-increasing light around the Earth, from Canada and the United States in the west, to Russia and India in the east, from Scandinavia in the north to South Africa and Botswana in the south.

In these diverse settings, Camphill has responded to the differing challenges of community-building, drawing on valuable past experience whilst remaining open to tackle new tasks with clarity and freshness.

Community-building, the 'social art', has no maps or blueprints. To walk into the unknown with others demands courage, creativity and trust - plus enormous reserves of humour! We have to work on ourselves, chiselling away the unnecessary and revealing the hidden form which appears only through great patience.

Essential, too, are those of us with special needs, so often the teachers and facilitators of new social forms, who inspire an ever-renewing vision of community which others can help to create and shape.

At the beginning of our journey we found the children with special needs whose care and education became the first responsibility of the Camphill Movement when it began over sixty years ago. These are the children who kindle warmth in our hearts and whose greatest need is the patience, creativity and faith of those around. These children remind us to keep mind and spirit active - for it is only our compassion and innovation which can change the world. Accepting this responsibility allows us to be touched by the Eternal Child within.

When Karl König witnessed his first Advent Garden he experienced how the arts in the service of a festival can transform and quicken the spirit and form bridges between individuals. Inspired by Karl König, the young Camphill Movement produced a journal called "The Cresset". A cresset is a sturdy vessel which contains the means to kindle a flame. The flame which the cresset of Camphill kindles is the flame of the child, the eternal child, the flame of art, of creativity. Ultimately, it is the flame of love.

Austria

Botswana

Canada

England

Estonia

France

Finland

Germany

India

Irish Republic

Northern
Ireland

The Netherlands

Norway

Poland

Russia

Scotland

South Africa

Sweden

Switzerland

USA

Wales

Acknowledgements

'shaping the flame' came about as a result of the enthusiastic participation and support of many people in the Camphill Movement in the United Kingdom and the Republic of Ireland.

Particular thanks must go to all the craftspeople and artists (past and present), many of whom have learning difficulties, who made workshops, studios and artwork available. Appreciation, too, to the Camphill Communities: Ballybay, Ballytobin, Beannacher, Blair Drummond, Botton Village, The Bridge, Camphill Rudolf Steiner Schools, Carrick-on-Suir, Cherry Orchards, Clanabogan, Coleg Elidyr, Corbenic, The Croft, Delrow, Camphill Devon, Duffcarig, Dunshane, Camphill East Anglia, Glencraig, The Grange, Grangemockler, Camphill Holywood, Kyle, Larchfield, Milltown, Camphill Milton Keynes, Mourne Grange, Newton Dee, Oaklands Park, Ochil Tower, Orchard Leigh, Pennine, Sheiling School Ringwood, Camphill St Albans, Simeon Care for the Elderly, Sturts Farm, Taurus Crafts, Templehill, Sheiling School Thornbury, Tigh a'Chomainn, Tiphereth, Thomastown. Also to Föhrenbühl Community in Germany, Humanus-Haus Community in Switzerland and Novalis House in South Africa.

Special thanks must also go to the Lantern, Glencraig and Loch Arthur Communities for giving the time for various individuals to be free to develop this book and to Camphill Houses, The Hatch, The Mount and William Morris House for hosting editorial group meetings.

We thank the Rudolf Steiner Press for permission to include verses by Rudolf Steiner. For the idea of linking the arts to the Christian Festivals we thank Sergei O. Prokofieff. The poems on the portrait page from *The saving life - an Anthology of poetry by Irish people with special needs*. Collected by Stuart Milson - Grangemockler Camphill. 1993.

Editorial Group

Bob Clay *(poetic text)*, Wain Farrants *(editing)*, Christopher Marshall *(project coordination)*, Boris Moscoff *(artistic direction)*, Lorraine Payne *(graphic design)*, Mimi Verhoeven *(artistic support)*.

Text Contributors

Descriptive text is by the editorial group with Sandy and Julia Cox. The text from page 12 to page 113 is by Bob Clay except where initials are shown at the foot of verses, as follows:

AB: Adam Bittleston; JB: Jimi Breen *(Page 113 "I Dunno")*; KK: Karl König; CAL: Christoph Andreas Lindenberg; RS: Rudolf Steiner; MT: Madeleine Thompson *(Page 112 "I can be good when I want to be")*; MV: Mimi Verhoeven.

Photographic Material

Keith Allardyce, Ruari Bennet, Paul Bock, Chester Music Limited, Nicholas Poole *(Botton Photo Archives)*, Stephen Rasch, Eric Schoetla, Mattias Spalinger and many others who kindly sent in selections from their communities.

Additional Contributions

Thanks also to Martin Astley *(Electrocolour Ltd)*, Charles Bamford *(Ringwood-Botton Eurythmy School)*, Claire Belbin, Freidwart Bock *(Karl König Library)*, Albertino Costa, Allmut ffrench, Bernard Graves *(Hiram Trust)*, Vivian Griffiths, Anthea Hailey *(Arion Lyre Association)*, Michael Hailey, Anne Harris OBE, Karin Herms, Michael Houston, Peter Howe *(Camphill Correspondence)*, Eta Ingham *(Trigonos)*, Bernard Jarman *(Biodynamic Agricultural Association)*, Kath Money, David Newbatt, Michael Odlin, Ian Parker, Andy Paton, Melanie Peacock, Cornelius Pietzner *(Carlo Pietzner Fund, for painting by George Kalmer)*, Wolodomyr Radysh *(Camphill Architects)*, Elena Riu, Henri van Rooij, Marga Schnell *(Hermann Gross Library)*, Martin Smith and colleagues *(Electrocolour Ltd)*, Val Street, John Tavener *(for the Foreword)*, Anne Walker, APT Creations of St Albans and to members of the Association of Camphill Communities and the Camphill Foundation.

Published in association with The Robinswood Press Stourbridge England.

Set in Matt Antique and Bellevue   Printed by Hill Shorter Ltd. West Bromwich England.

Information on Camphill can be obtained from The Association of Camphill Communities. Telephone: 01653 694197
Address: Gawain House 56 Welham Road Norton Malton North Yorkshire YO17 9DP   www.camphill.co.uk

Reading List

Festivals, Family and Food.
Diana Carey and Judy Large (Hawthorn Press)

The Art of Living.
Veronica van Duin (Kate Roth Publications)

*A Guide to Camphill Communities
in the United Kingdom and the Republic of Ireland*
Edited by Michael Hailey
(Association of Camphill Communities)

*Education for Special Needs:
Principles and Practice in Camphill*
Henning Hansmann (Floris Books)

Brothers and Sisters
Karl König (Floris Books)

Children with Special Needs
Michael Luxford (Floris Books)

Karl König, A Twentieth Century Biography
Hans Mueller-Wiedemann (Camphill Books)

A Candle on the Hill: Images of Camphill Life
Edited by Cornelius Pietzner (Floris Books)

*Living Buildings: An Expression of Fifty Years of
Camphill Halls and Chapels of the Camphill Movement*
Joan de Ris Allen (Camphill Architects)

The Festivals and Their Meaning.
Rudolf Steiner (Rudolf Steiner Press)

Verses and Meditations
Rudolf Steiner (Rudolf Steiner Press)

Eurythmy - an Art of Movement for Our Time
Shaina Stoehr (The Robinswood Press)

A Man Before Others - Rudolf Steiner Remembered
(Rudolf Steiner Press)